BRITISH COLUMBIA

A SYMPHONY IN COLOR

Text by
G. E. Mortimore

Collins Toronto

Captain James Cook, R.N., often wears a seagull or a pigeon for a hat as he surveys the Empress Hotel with bronze eyes from his pedestal on the Causeway of Victoria's Inner Harbor. The insolent birds perched on the statue are a reminder of the small importance of human heroes in a province where the true central character is the land.

Stretching 500 miles east and nearly 800 miles north and northwest of Victoria's legislative dome and Vancouver's corporate towers and mansions, are the huge territories from which flow the timber, mineral, petroleum, fishery and hydro electric wealth that built these recent human structures.

No map or tourist brochure can show the real shape and color of British Columbia. It takes many personal journeys to experience and begin to understand 366,255 square miles of fir, spruce and pine forest slopes, high rocky summits, glaciers, alpine meadows, deserts, rain forests, plateau ranchlands, orchards, northern prairie wheatfields, alluvial valleys, great rivers and lakes and thousands of creeks and streams; sleeping volcanoes, hot springs and island-studded coastlines with wide beaches and mountain cliffs plunging into fjords overlooked by snowy peaks.

This regional empire is Canada's furthest west and third largest province. British Columbia is bounded to the south by the United States border, which runs along the forty-ninth parallel of latitude and down the middle of Georgia Strait, Haro Strait and the Strait of Juan de Fuca; to the east by Alberta, including a section of the Rocky Mountain Continental Divide; to the north by the Yukon Territory along the sixtieth parallel; and to the west by the Alaska Panhandle and the Pacific Ocean. B.C. is bigger than Britain and France together. It could contain the states of Washington, Oregon, California, Rhode Island, Connecticut, Massachusetts, New Hampshire and Vermont. Vancouver Island, on which Victoria, the capital, stands, is larger than Wales and almost half as large as Ireland.

The mosaic of landforms, climates and communities that is now called B.C. was shaped by four sequences of events: the geological upheavals of the earth's crust 136 to 25 million years ago which created the mountains that dominate B.C.'s surface; the advances and retreats of the glaciers, culminating in the last ice age 20,000 to 10,000 years ago, which covered the land with a sheet of ice as much as a mile deep; the occupation of the land and sea coast, after the retreat of the ice, by successive waves of people now called Indians who crossed from Asia when Bering Strait was dry land; and the European invasion of the last two centuries.

Vancouver these pages *originated in the 1870s as a sawmilling settlement called Granville. It was renamed Vancouver after Captain George Vancouver of the Royal Navy who had navigated the coast in 1792. The residential area alongside Kitsilano Beach is pictured left, while above is a view of the Grouse Mountain Sky Ride. An ocean liner leaves the port top, and two superb views of the city can be seen opposite page top and bottom.*
Overleaf A magnificent photograph of Vancouver's magical night-time skyline.

Vancouver these pages is a densely populated city, located on the southwestern edge of British Columbia. It is set in a spectacular landscape which incorporates the wild mountain country of the Coast Range to the north, gentle rolling farmlands and, of course, the Burrard Inlet, a natural harbor around which the city is built. Vancouver is Canada's third largest city and the pulsating business heart of British Columbia. The new high-rise buildings of Vancouver's West End can be seen facing page below *from Vanier Park, and set in the park itself is the H R MacMillan Planetarium* facing page top.

Overleaf *The Lions Gate Bridge, just under a mile long, was opened in 1938. Here it can be seen silhouetted against a dusky evening sky, as the city's lights begin to sparkle in the twilight.*

The Europeans, propelled outward by a complex series of social explosions and transformations in their home countries, spilled across the globe from the sixteenth century onward. However, it was not until the eighteenth century that they got a foothold in what is now British Columbia. The Russians, pushing across northern seas to Alaska, as they had previously thrust their land empire across Siberia, were the first Europeans on the northwest coast. Britain and Spain hurried to answer the challenge; but Spain dropped out quite early.

Less than three human lifetimes ago, the first European exploring and trading ships were sailing into harbor; and land-based fur traders and explorers were paddling and scrambling laboriously through the wilder-ness of British Columbia, re-discovering paths that the Indians had already discovered and re-naming places that the Indians had already named.

Some people who were born in 1778, the year Captain Cook sailed into Nootka Sound on Vancouver Island's west coast, or in 1792, the year Captain George Vancouver, R.N., mapped the coast and circled the island that bears his name, or in 1793, when Alexander Mackenzie pushed west by land to the Pacific – lived long enough to see most of the crucial events that shaped B.C. In one long lifetime, two separate British colonies grew and merged together and (in 1871) joined as a province in a new nation called Canada.

Before the European invasion some 80,000 Indians

Queen Elizabeth Park, originally called Little Mountain Park, covers an area of 130 acres and provides an oasis within the city of Vancouver. It was built on the site of an abandoned rock quarry, which is now well hidden under smooth green lawns interwoven with winding paths. It boasts a glorious Rose Garden, a Sunken Garden above center, an Arboretum and the brilliantly colorful 75th Anniversary Gardens. It is also the site of the unique Bloedel Conservatory above left and right, right, and facing page, where three separate climatic zones are found under one vast dome. In simulated desert, rain forest and tropical weather, some 400 species of exotic plants and flowers thrive.
Overleaf Vancouver seen from Vanier Park.

lived in British Columbia. On the coast, a relatively dense population with an efficient tool kit and a rich array of heraldic art used the potlatch system of ritual feasts for validating names and property and distributing food, social status and treasures in a way that smoothed out surpluses and scarcities through local and regional interchanges. On the inland plateau, people based on the upper reaches of salmon rivers followed a wider yearly food-getting round. In the arctic drainage, caribou-hunting Athapascans spaced themselves out across enormous areas of land. Pre-European trade routes linked the three zones.

The fur trade at first enriched the B.C. Indians with many new tools, paints, weapons and foods, and touched off a burst of intensified ritual, trade and warfare; but epidemics of European diseases killed tens of thousands of people, while a rush of gold-miners, settlers, railway-builders, miners of coal and industrial metals, loggers and manufacturers, pushed the native people aside and deprived them of their land. Yet except for small patches of land in the southwest and northeast, none of B.C. was even conditionally ceded by treaty. Native people insist that B.C. still morally and legally belongs to them.

Today, instead of 80,000 people living in a dynamic balance with nature, there are 2,710,000 people linked up with world wide channels of trade and political power. More than half are crowded into the urban southwest: 1,150,000 in Greater Vancouver and 250,000 in Greater Victoria.

How do you get a grip on such a complex reality as British Columbia? A good starting point is the Provincial Museum in Victoria, where you can walk through a total-

The Lions Gate Bridge left was built to provide access to the new development of West and North Vancouver across the Burrard Inlet. Two very different views of downtown Vancouver can be seen right and bottom: one is a view from New Courthouse overlooking Robson Square; the other is at night, across False Creek. Leading to downtown Vancouver and Robson Street is busy Cambie Street opposite page below right, seen here in rush hour. In the 1950s, Germans and other European immigrants opened continental shops and cafés on Robson Street – and it became known as Robson Strasse. An extraordinary view of the Planetarium is shown opposite page below left.

Overleaf A view of Vancouver.

experience exhibit that condenses 20,000 years and 366,255 square miles into a tour that can last thirty minutes or a week. The next step could be the kind of god's-eye overview that comes from taking the measure of B.C.'s two extremes. First, pass rapidly through the part that has changed the most since the Europeans came – the urban southwest. Then fly up to the part that has changed the least – B.C.'s sparsely peopled great north – and return for a region-by-region journey of discovery.

From the Provincial Museum it is a short walk to a seaplane base. There you can go on a thirty-five minute harbor-to-harbor flight that carries you over the Gulf Islands to Vancouver. On this time-scale, Victoria and Vancouver are two ends of the same city. The low-lying cherry blossoms and granite of the political-administrative capital appear in closely linked contrast to the steel, glass and concrete, the bustling traffic and overshadowing coastal mountains of Vancouver, which is B.C.'s commercial and industrial metropolis.

Across Lions' Gate Bridge it is a twenty minute drive to the foot of Grouse Mountain, where a gondola car lifts you up to the ski slopes and a cliff-edge restaurant where you can sip B.C. wine and eat B.C. salmon while you watch the sun set over the strait beyond the anchored ships. Thousands of lights stretch down the slopes of the North Shore, across and beyond the Fraser River and its flat delta lands to the United States border, marking the extent of Canada's largest seaport (in cargo volume) its growing zone of industry and commerce and suburban sprawl, and its web of transportation routes radiating in every direction.

If your timing is right, you may be able to descend the mountain and drive to the airport within the hour for a flight to Prince George.

THE GREAT NORTH

B.C.'s great north is the half of the province that lies between the fifty-fourth parallel and the Yukon border. Mackenzie moved south and west from here to the coast. Simon Fraser, following in his footsteps, founded Fort St. James on Stuart Lake in 1806 as one of a chain of forts designed to intercept the furs that were flowing from inland Indians to their coastal Indian trading partners, and thence to the American trading ships.

Prince George was a fur trade fort; now it is B.C.'s third largest city, with a population of 70,000. It lies near the geographical center of the province. The fur traders did a lot of meandering and back-tracking before they learned their way around. A short distance north of Prince George is the divide between the Pacific and Arctic oceans' drainage systems. The Peace River flows east through the Rockies and eventually drains into the northward-flowing Mackenzie River. Alexander Mackenzie blundered along the waterways down to the Arctic Ocean before he found a route to the Pacific. Simon Fraser in 1808 canoed and portaged the perilous rapids and canyons to the mouth of the river that now bears his name. It turned out to be the wrong river. He thought he was descending the Columbia.

Fort St. James has been rebuilt as a historical replica. It was one of two anchor points for the western part of the fur trade empire. The southern headquarters was at the mouth of the Columbia. Fraser named the northern sector New Caledonia, in honor of his parents' home country, Scotland. Because there already was a French colony named New Caledonia, Queen Victoria later renamed the

By night, Vancouver takes on a unique sequined, sparkling beauty. A view of Water Street in trendy Gastown above *looks towards the Harbour Centre Building; from the Royal Vancouver Yacht Club, across Coal Harbour, can be seen the panorama* left; *and* above left *is an aerial view of the Hotel Vancouver in the center of the city. On the opposite page* are illustrated *the Old Courthouse Fountain in Robson Square* top left; *an exotic modern sculpture in front of Eaton's Pacific Centre* top right; *the glamorous foyer of the Orpheum Theatre* bottom left; *and the Orpheum's elegant auditorium* bottom right.

Overleaf *A night view of the city seen across Coal Harbour.*

territory British Columbia.

A triangle of roads and railways encloses the north; several road and rail spurs plunge into the wilderness heartland; and fly-in planes can drop fishermen at remote lakes. Even the adventurers who travel on foot are equipped with an industrial society's aids to survival: rifles, maps, radios, lightweight sleeping bags; but you still have to be careful. Carry extra gas, spare parts, food, axe, matches and sleeping bags when you drive northern roads. Consult experienced guides and outfitters and tell someone your timetable before you hike into the wilderness. It is still possible to get lost and starve.

The baseline of the transportation triangle is the road-rail corridor that runs through Yellowhead Pass in the Rockies, through Prince George to the seaport of Prince Rupert. The second leg is the 613-mile B.C. section of the Alaska Highway. This 1,523-mile highway is an engineering marvel. Ten thousand American soldiers and 6,000 Canadian civilians drove it through mountains and muskeg in ten months in 1942. The western leg is the Stewart-Cassiar Highway, which runs from Terrace on the Skeena River to join the Alaska Highway just inside the Yukon.

The northeastern Peace River Block is B.C.'s only slice of the prairies. The region around Dawson Creek and Fort St. John is becoming B.C.'s major energy center. Pipelines and transmission lines carry Peace River natural gas and hydro electric power to Vancouver. New Peace River coal mines are being developed for export markets.

The village of 'Ksan near Hazelton is an important

center in the current re-awakening of northwest coast Indian art and legend. Here, in great houses bearing the crests of the clans and lineages of the Gitksan, visitors can see carvers and painters at work re-creating northwest coast cultural treasures.

Natural wonders include the hot springs of the Liard, the volcanic cones of Mount Edziza Provincial Park, and the unspoiled uplands of Spatsizi Plateau Wilderness Provincial Park.

The complex geology of B.C.'s mountain chains is gradually yielding its mineral wealth: Feverish episodes of

Horseshoe Bay above left serves as a ferry port for travelers to Vancouver Island. Point Atkinson Lighthouse above is seen here against a perfect blue sky; and the coastal scenery around Vancouver top has all the romance and variety to captivate even the most seasoned traveler. Kitsilano

Beach and swimming pool right – a summer playground for residents and tourists alike. Brightly decked-out boats are reflected in the waters of the Royal Vancouver Yacht Club top right, set in Stanley Park.

Overleaf A night view of the city looking across False Creek.

gold-mining in Atlin, Omineca and Cassiar; copper at Stewart, asbestos at Cassiar, molybdenum at Kitsault. Some of these industries have guided tours for the public. B.C. Hydro at the W.A.C. Bennett Dam on the Peace River has a public information program which includes tours of the powerhouse and a museum of fossils and life-size models of dinosaurs.

Despite these friendly gestures, the great north is B.C.'s major environmental battleground. There is a continuing struggle between developers and defenders over the environmental and social damage that may be caused by proposed new mines, dams and pipelines.

THE GREAT TRANSFORMATION

It makes a puzzle to think about as you fly south: How do you read the balance-sheet of gains and losses from the industrial transformation of the wilderness?

The W.A.C. Bennett Dam has created a man-made lake larger than any natural body of fresh water. In a province where agricultural and grazing land is barely ten percent of the total, substantial amounts of farm land have

In British Columbia downhill skiing is an extremely popular sport, and the province's largest ski area is at Whistler Mountain. Whistler Ski Village facing page below *is a new and very luxurious ski resort. The photographs these pages were taken at the Molson World Downhill 1982. The fireworks display* far right *is a spectacular event which takes place the night before the race. On the day, all the competitors ski down the run carrying the flags of their own nations* facing page top. *The winner, Peter Mueller of Switzerland, and the runner up, Canadian Steve Podborski, can be seen* right *waving at the crowd while* above right *people flock to watch the prize-giving ceremony.*

been flooded by dams, and more is threatened. Seventy percent of the marshes at the mouth of the Fraser have been diked and filled, making new land but destroying vital fresh-water habitat for salmon. Victoria's Empress Hotel occupies filled land on the site of tidal James Bay. Roads, railways, pipelines and air routes girdle the province from end to end.

The face of B.C. is partly a human artifact; and yet terrain and climate remain decisive factors in the making of events. In such a rugged country, it costs a lot to bring the logs and minerals out.

The western world's expanding hunger for energy and raw materials fuelled the twentieth-century drive to exploit the resources of B.C.'s wilderness. B.C.'s economy has recently been diversified by the addition of new manufacturing plants; but the province's continued high degree of dependence on the export of raw or lightly processed minerals and forest products still influences

B.C.'s steeply wavering booms and depressions.

B.C.'s industrial expansion of the 1950s to the 1980s is the latest in a series of spurts of growth that dates back a century. In 1858, thousands of whiskered, red-shirted miners with revolvers and bowie knives at their belts arrived to seek their fortunes in a Fraser River gold rush which made Victoria a boom town and opened the way for a mass invasion of settlers. James Douglas, the tall, sturdy man who was both governor of Vancouver Island and Chief Factor for the Hudson's Bay Company, was ready for the gold rush. Because of the way that history moulded the leaders of the fur trade, his career had been a rehearsal for this event.

Most of the miners were European-American frontier adventurers. The infiltration of American settlers had lost for Britain the Hudson's Bay Company fur trading territories between the mouth of the Columbia River and the forty-ninth parallel (the present state of Washington).

The exciting photographs these pages were taken during the "Molson World Downhill 1982." Clearing air above is a competitor who has just negotiated a treacherous swirl of a bend which is aptly named the "Toilet Bowl"!

The photographs top left, top right and facing page below were all taken from the same spot, where the skiers move swiftly over a stretch called the "Meadows" on their way to the "Elevator Shaft." The Canadian competitors are easy to spot in their distinctive yellow racing colors top right and facing page top. Cheering spectators line the route as Steve Podborski sweeps past the finishing gate marked by two red banners facing page top, in a time which will eventually win him a prize for being the second-fastest skier to complete the run, just behind Peter Mueller.

A multi-colored forest of skis planted in deep snow left indicates that a large number of the competitors are enjoying a well-earned drink in the pub.

In 1843, when Douglas was an officer of the company at Fort Vancouver on the Columbia, he had travelled north and founded Fort Victoria, because of a fear that American claims to Washington would be recognized by treaty. In 1846, the fear came true. Fort Victoria replaced Fort Vancouver (now Vancouver, Wash.) as the company's main Pacific depot.

Douglas wanted to make sure that the Americans would not take over B.C. as they had taken over Washington. Seizing policy in his own hands, he proclaimed that the gold belonged to the Crown. Miners would have to buy licences. Officially he had no jurisdiction in mainland B.C., but the government in London later approved his action.

Gold commissioners, magistrates, judges, police, soldiers, road-builders and warships imposed British-style law and order and opened a controlled flow of goods and communication. The Union Jack continued to fly north of forty-nine, while more than 30,000 miners from California, Oregon and Washington crowded in to extract $25 million worth of gold in seven years from the gravel bars and creeks of the Fraser and the Cariboo country.

Douglas and most other noted figures in B.C. history were officers of large organizations: The Royal Navy, the Northwest Company, the Hudson's Bay Company, the Canadian Pacific Railway, the B.C. government. They also were wheeler-dealers who acted decisively before orders could be received from distant headquarters or a mandate conferred by a scattered electorate. They were raised in a society that rewarded a balance of obedience and bold

Pacific Rim National Park these pages *is situated on the west coast of Vancouver Island. It stretches from Port Renfrew to Tofino, and one of its most outstanding features is Long Beach* this page *and* opposite page below. *The park is divided into three main sections: Long Beach, a section which not only covers* the coastline but also the rain forests opposite page top left and right; *Barkley Sound, including the Broken Islands Group; and the West Coast Trail, a wilderness between Bamfield and Port Renfrew. The trail itself was established for shipwrecked sailors who could walk inland and find this pathway to civilization!*

action. Douglas was a stickler for ceremony. Everything had to be correct, down to the last gold thread in his uniform. When he retired at sixty as Sir James Douglas, KCB, he went on the Grand Tour of Europe that heirs of upper-class and wealthy families had taken since the eighteenth century. Men usually began the tour before age twenty. But Douglas had been busy for forty-five years helping to build an empire. Now he embarked on a furiously active year of cathedral viewing, art gallery visiting and educational sightseeing.

VICTORIA

Near the place where Governor Douglas used to ride out on horseback from his house, English double-decker buses, lumbering horse-drawn tally-hos and harbor cruise boats wait to pick up passengers for guided tours.

Tourism has changed since Douglas went on his Grand Tour. The "Englishness" of Victoria is founded on history; but today it is more than history. It has become theater. The English thread is woven into the fabric of a

A selection of Indian and Indian-influenced sculpture: right *an Indian mask in the Provincial Museum within Victoria's Heritage Court Complex;* far right and below far right *totem poles in Stanley Park, Vancouver;* below right *sculpture in Robson Square, Vancouver;* bottom and left *exhibits in the University of British Columbia's Museum of Anthropology, Vancouver; and* below *a Kwakiutl heraldic pole in Thunderbird Park, Victoria.*

romantic entertainment package designed for the tourists, which includes a street of replicas of historic English houses, put together by the late Sam Lane at his Olde England Inn; undersea aquariums, indoor tropical gardens, waxworks, car museums, a brightly refurbished Chinatown; and a distinguished array of restaurants, antique dealers, wool, china and chocolate shops; and boutiques of international reputation where you can buy art objects, clothing and utensils from India, South America, the Northwest Coast and the Canadian Arctic.

Victoria's mild, sunny climate makes a good home for garden plants from every continent. A highlight among the city's attractions is Butchart's Gardens on outlying Tod Inlet, where a cement magnate and his wife transformed a quarry into a year-round festival of flowers. The package includes the chimes of a Dutch carillon, the bells of Christ Church Cathedral, Jerry Gosley's Smile Show and a summer musical production, "The Wonder of It All," based on the life of Victoria painter and writer, Emily Carr. Her dark, swirling canvasses, full of the mystery of the forest, now command thousands of dollars; but she lived much of her life in such poverty that she sometimes had to work with house paints on cheap wrapping paper.

A blend of exclusiveness and hospitality forms part of Victoria's character. In colonial days the autocratic Douglas made political alliances with some of the younger sons of good English and Irish families and impoverished gentry who came out to supervise the Hudson's Bay Company's farming operations and staff the civil service. However, there were snobs who called him "Old Square-Toes" and sniggered at the attempts of the

In the city of Victoria is a charming little area called the "Olde English Village" left. The Olde Curiosity Shoppe sells gifts and souvenirs, and there are perfect replicas of Anne Hathaway's cottage and garden and Shakespeare's birthplace. On display are sixteenth century furniture and utensils, a lace-making device, trenchers and even a man-trap. Traditional English foods, like roast beef and Yorkshire pudding, or proper afternoon teas tempt the visitor to linger awhile. Victoria is British Columbia's capital, and both the city and its people are mainly of British origin.

Boats are gathered in Victoria's harbor below in preparation for the annual "Swift Sure" yacht race. In the evening, they are overlooked by the beautifully illuminated Parliament Buildings facing page top and bottom. Historic Wippletree Junction below left offers antiques and souvenirs of bygone days.

Douglas' daughters to manage fashionable clothes sent from London.

B.C.'s provincial government, centered in Francis M. Rattenbury's turn-of-the-century granite Legislative Buildings, has a legislature that is modelled on the parliament in London. It preserves some of the symbols of ancient privilege along with hard-won democratic rights. Laws are made in the name of the Crown as embodied in the federally-appointed Lieutenant-Governor; but they result from decisions made by the party that commands the majority of elected members in the legislature. In practice these decisions are made behind closed doors by the cabinet (which is the executive committee of the

government) and the majority party's caucus; then they are debated and passed in the House.

Some cynics say that many of the important decisions are made in the Union Club, an unmarked haunt of the monied elite. Across Humboldt Street from the club is the hearty, low-class Beaver Bar, which occupies the northwest corner of the Empress, sealed off with a separate entrance, to discourage beer-drinking common people from entering the hotel.

THE ISLANDS AND THE COAST

·Vancouver Island is the biggest of 6,500 islands that lie along the B.C. coast. The province has 16,900 miles of deeply convoluted coastline. Vancouver Island and the Queen Charlotte Islands are the above-water part of B.C.'s westernmost mountain chain, separated from the mainland by an undersea trench.

A coastal tour confronts you with the province's three main geographical facts: sea, mountains and forest. The Japan current offshore keeps the coast relatively warm. Moisture-laden winds sweeping over varied heights of land dump their loads in amounts that differ from place to place: 26 to 46 inches of rainfall in Victoria, varying from district to district; 50 to 70 in Vancouver; 120 on the island's west coast; 172 on the mainland at Ocean Falls.

This mosaic of mini-climates, which stimulated eco-nomic exchange between zones, probably was one reason for the dense population and high culture of native Indians. Another reason was the abundant food provided by the enormous number of Pacific salmon, which grow to maturity in the sea and run up the rivers to spawn and die. In Victoria's Provincial Museum and Thunderbird Park, you can see the differing art styles of the three cultural-ecological regions of B.C. Coast Indians: the Salish of the south; the Kwakiutl and Nootka of the central zone; and the Tsimshian and Haida of the north. The government hired Kwakiutl wise man, Mungo Martin, and other artists to carve poles and build a Kwakiutl house; but a proposal to preserve the vanishing treasures of Indian languages is perennially raised and ignored in the legislature.

The absolutely magnificent gardens illustrated on these pages were once a quarry for Robert Pim Butchart's cement plant! In 1904 Mr. and Mrs. Butchart decided to transform the bleak quarry, and began by planting a few roses and sweet peas. From this small beginning grew a dedicated and expensive hobby, as the Butcharts began to collect flowers and plants from all over the world. The Sunken Garden was transformed into a great bowlful of color, which overflowed into the Rose Garden, the Italian Garden and the Japanese Garden. They named their gardens "Benvenuto," the Italian word for "Welcome," and everyone is welcome to come and enjoy the wonderful Butchart Gardens. Over half a million photographs are taken here annually, and the gardens feature blooms of every season.
Overleaf *Cottonwood House near Quesnel.*

You can go by rail as far as Courtenay, or drive from Victoria to Port Hardy at the island's north end, drive aboard a ferry that will carry you through the sheltered channels of the inside passage to Prince Rupert, then change ferries to cross stormy Hecate Strait to the Queen Charlottes. Finally, you and your car can go down to Vancouver by sea.

Much of the route lies through territories controlled by lumber and pulp and paper companies, who hold the land on forest management licences. Ninety-five percent of B.C.'s surface is publicly owned Crown land. Big business and big government are salient features of today's social landscape. Of the thousands of individualists who reject the centralized, bureaucratic life, many can be found on the Gulf Islands. Some of them bring their carving, weaving, pottery and organic foods each year to Courtenay's Renaissance Fair, one of a circuit of small-is-beautiful celebrations throughout the province. Noted Indian crafts of the region are the Cowichan sweaters knitted from raw wool at Duncan (Prince Charles and Lady Diana got Cowichan sweaters for wedding presents) and the Haida slate carvings of the Queen Charlottes, which are in the price bracket of Inuit (Eskimo) carvings.

Some of the places worth visting are the railway and logging-equipment museum at Duncan; the one remaining bastion of the old Hudson's Bay Company fort at

The old gold town of Barkerville this page: *St. Saviours Anglican Church* right and top left *sits at the end of the main street; while* left *is shown the printing office of the "Cariboo Sentinel," and* below right *The Barkerville Hotel. A general impression of Main Street can be seen* below left. Facing page *the excitement of the annual Prince George Professional Rodeo.* Overleaf *Evening draws in over Lillooet Lake.*

Nanaimo; one of B.C.'s last stands of readily accessible virgin timber, including an 800-year-old Douglas fir, nine feet through, at MacMillan Park on the road to Port Alberni; Pacific Rim National Park near Tofino, where the waves of the open Pacific come crashing in on the sands of Long Beach; and the museum owned by the Cape Mudge band of Kwakiutl Indians on Quadra Island.

The Haidas of the Queen Charlottes were notable warriors and traders who travelled hundreds of miles in their seagoing canoes. Once they numbered some 8,000, but smallpox nearly wiped them out. Most of their villages were abandoned. The forest grew around the fallen beams of the great painted houses and the half-crumbled leaning mortuary poles. One of the abandoned villages, Ninstints on Anthony Island, is now a World Heritage Site ranking with the pyramids and Chartres Cathedral. To land there, you need the permission of B.C. Parks and the Skidegate Indian Band.

Some Queen Charlottes people resent the traffic that came with an improved ferry service. Don't be surprised if you find a truck parked in the middle of a narrow bridge, leaving you no room to pass. Some islanders just don't like outside visitors; happily others do.

VANCOUVER

World-wide economic forces caused the tiny isolated mill town of Granville to explode into an "instant metropolis" much as a volcano grew out of a Mexican cornfield. That is the way historian Howard White, editor of *Raincoast Chronicles*, sums up the rise of Vancouver out of

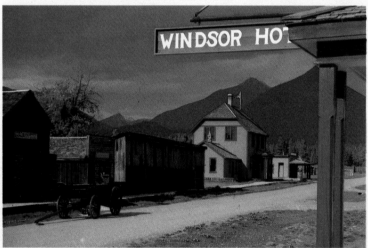

Situated in the Fort Steele Historic Park is a reconstructed Kootenay town of the 1890-1905 period. Fort Steele above, right, top right and opposite page top was a ghost town after World War II, and literally came back to life in the 1960s. Center right *The*

CN Railway crossing the North Thompson River. Opposite page below *Three Valley Gap frontier town near Revelstoke.*

Overleaf *A sawmill on the shore of Lake Slocan near Nelson.*

the forest in less than a century.

Almost every street commands a different long distance sea or mountain view in the multi-level city that straddles Burrard Inlet and the Fraser delta. From the mountain slopes and tall buildings, past the loungers and street musicians, to the bustle of Granville Market, Vancouver is a city of dazzling contrast in height and

Yoho National Park right *is a wilderness of wild valleys, towering mountains and glaciers, waterfalls and lakes. Yoho is set in the heart of the Canadian Rockies and adjoins Banff National Park on its eastern boundary and Kootenay National Park on its southern one. Running through the middle of the park is the turbulent Kicking Horse River – named after a bad-tempered pack-horse which kicked the geologist and physician, Sir James Hector, during the Palliser Expedition in 1858. Bowron Lake below is set in Bowron Lakes Provincial Park in the Cariboo, a magnificent wilderness area famous for its 72 mile canoe circuit and its wildlife sanctuary. In Wells Gray Park, which has many good hiking trails, can be found the spectacular Helmcken Falls* below right; *while at mile 456 of the Alaska Highway is Muncho Lake* facing page.

Overleaf *Howe Sound and Lions Bay near Squamish.*

social position. It has a theatrical quality. You go about the streets feeling like a minor actor in a David Lean film.

Through Vancouver's brief history loggers, industrialists and tourist operators have been busy translating the scenery into dollars.

Large stands of easily accessible big trees drew lumbermen to Burrard Inlet in the 1860s. Most of present-day Greater Vancouver was forest, stumps and marshes, when John "Gassy Jack" Deighton built a saloon for thirsty loggers near the shacktown of Stamps' Mill in 1867. A hamlet called Granville, or Gastown, grew up around the hotel. Ten miles away, a detachment of Royal Engineers in 1859 had cut a hole in the forest to build New

Westminster, which became for a time the capital of British Columbia. Fourteen miles up the Fraser from there, the Hudson's Bay Company had built Fort Langley in 1827 as a major Pacific base; but when the company learned that great sections of the river were too rough to navigate, the fort became a secondary depot. It has been reconstructed as a historical replica.

After the newly-completed Canadian Pacific Railway had been extended from Port Moody to Vancouver, the first scheduled transcontinental train reached Vancouver in 1887, making the city an important link in an expanding network of world trade. Vancouver's rapid growth dates from that time. The city became a supply depot for the Klondike gold rush and for the gold, silver, copper, lead, zinc and coal mines of the B.C. interior. The growing seaport handled silk and tea from China and Japan, and prairie grain and B.C. salmon, lumber and minerals going out to world markets.

Here in British Columbia, vast regions of virtual wilderness are to be found, all protected by British Columbians themselves, people who take deep pride in their environment. The B.C. Forest Service, alongside other conservationists, has worked hard to reclothe the landscape in its natural woodland cover, for much of it was indiscriminately cleared by the forest industry. Over 100 million seedlings are planted annually, and harvesting is, in general, restricted to government-designated areas. As each area is cleared, so it is replanted. The lakeside scenery is, perhaps, the loveliest: opposite page bottom right is Pavillion Lake near Lillooet, and right is Burns Lake. The blossoming orchards facing page top enhance the Okanagan Valley each spring.

Thanks to the foresight of Vancouver's first city council (1886) the city has 1,000 acres of wooded park near downtown. Vancouver's attractions include Stanley Park's zoo and aquarium with its performing killer whales and dolphins; the Centennial Museum, Maritime Museum (counterpart to the B.C. Maritime Museum in Victoria); MacMillan Planetarium, University of British Columbia's Museum of Anthropology, Bloedel Conservatory of tropical plants; an extensive Chinatown; the cosmopolitan shopping district of Robson Street in the residential-commercial West End; and the boutiques and restaurants of Gastown, the city's revitalized historic core.

Vancouver and Victoria are gateways to a world of learning, arts and amusements. Both cities have universities, theater companies, symphony orchestras and art galleries. Within a short distance of both major cities are playgrounds for skiers, hikers, mountain climbers, golfers, cave explorers, canoeists, river

raftsmen, fishermen, yachtsmen, scuba-divers, hunters, bird-watchers, rockhounds, amateur botanists and gourmet food hobbyists.

The cities are headquarters and taking-off places for a procession of events which include Vancouver's Sea Festival and Pacific National Exhibition; Victoria's Swiftsure yacht classic; the open house that is held at intervals at Victoria's Esquimalt naval base; Nanaimo's annual bathtub race; outhouse races at Creston and Lac La Hache; and a catalogue of regattas, rodeos, stampedes, loggers' sports, fairs and festivals of fruit and flowers.

CENTRAL B.C.

The heart of B.C. is the 90,000-square-mile drainage system of the Fraser River, which is one quarter of the province. The Fraser defines central B.C. To the north is the Arctic Ocean drainage; to the west are the smaller streams flowing into the Pacific; to the southeast is B.C.'s share of the Columbia's watershed.

The Fraser washed down the placer gold that attracted the miners; then it provided the rough and dangerous highway that led them inland to the deeper-buried bonanza of the Cariboo. Stern-wheel steamboats pushed up the river carrying miners and supplies until they reached impassible rapids and narrows. The miners continued by one of two routes. Some took a land-and-water short cut from Harrison Lake to Lillooet. Others scratched their way along the perilous cliffs of the Fraser Canyon. A number of miners and pack mules died when they slipped and fell to the river more than 1,000 feet below.

In Mount Robson Provincial Park above *the mountain looms behind Robson River; blue skies are reflected in Slocan Lake* above left; *sunlight dapples the hillsides around Kamloops Lake* right; *and the Skeena River runs between pine-clad shores* above right. Overleaf *A view of the Fraser River taken near Lillooet.*

Governor Douglas had roads built on both routes. The Harrison Lake route fell into disuse, but Highway 1, the Trans-Canada Highway, still follows Douglas's cliff-hanging wagon road. Two transcontinental railways also follow the river. Harrison Hot Springs, where the steamboats used to pass by with loads of miners bound for Lillooet, is now a resort community near the reputed home of that legendary eight-foot-tall human-like monster, the Sasquatch. Like Ogopogo, the lake serpent of the Okanagan, the Sasquatch is a fragment clipped out of context from the web of Indian cautionary tales and mysteries that dramatise the dangers of the environment and man's close link with nature. Sasquatch has been put to work as a commercial tourist monster. But does he really exist? Some people believe that he does, and have written books to prove it.

Travelling conditions in the canyon have improved since Simon Fraser and his men inched along with the aid of an Indian-built network of ropes. Now you can get out of your car and ride an aerial tram across Hell's Gate, where the Fraser narrows to 200 feet. From Jackass Mountain you can look down 2,000 feet to the river.

Highway 1 veers east through the beef-cattle center and one-time fur-trade post of Kamloops. The sagebrush semi-desert here and in the nearby Okanagan has a

rainfall of less than ten inches a year in some places. The old Cariboo Road, running north past log houses and cattle ranches, is now called Highway 97.

At Barkerville, a reconstructed version of the Cariboo's most famous gold-rush town draws thousands of visitors. Here the stubborn English sailor Billy Barker followed a hunch and (ignoring the jeers of fellow-miners who said he was crazy) dug fifty-two feet down to the ancient bed of Williams Creek and found a rich gold-bearing layer. He spent his fortune on his new wife and in the taverns of Barkerville, and died broke in Victoria.

From Williams Lake you can drive or ride the bus through the Chilcotin country to Bella Coola, where Mackenzie reached salt water.

THE SOUTHEAST

Adjoining the Fraser's drainage basin is the south-eastern section of mountains and valleys that sends its snow-melt and rainwater down to join the Columbia River. The Columbia's watershed includes the sunny, fruit-growing Okanagan and the lakes and mineral-rich mountains of the Kootenays.

In 1862, fifteen years after the last fur brigades had passed along the route from the mouth of the Columbia, Rev. Father Charles Pandosy planted the first apple tree in the mission grounds near Kelowna. Now fruit trees grown with irrigation water on the arid slopes above Okanagan Lake yield a crop worth $100 millions a year. Pick-it-yourself orchards and roadside fruit stands provide a succession of cherries, apricots, peaches, plums, pears and apples, while in a small cottage winery standing among its vineyards high on the slope above Okanagan Lake, the owners will pour you a sample or two of their vintages and sell you a bottle of a choice private brand.

In the northern part of this region, Highway 1 from Kamloops runs parallel to the route that was blasted through by the Canadian Pacific Railway. In the south, Highway 3 runs from the Fraser through the Okanagan and the Kootenays into Alberta. Icefields, hot springs, ski resorts and large areas of national and provincial parks stretch along these southeastern borders.

At Grand Forks is the Doukhobor Museum, honoring the people who came to Canada to escape religious persecution in Tsarist Russia.

The prosperous lead-zinc smelter at Trail is the last survivor among six smelters that used to process the ores of this region. All through the Kootenays are deserted ghost mining towns. A chain of hydro electric dams on the Columbia and its tributaries provides power on both sides of the border. B.C.'s first hydro power was generated on Cottonwood Creek near Nelson. After a mineral boom, Nelson went through a period of slow growth. This froze the town's appearance as it was in the boom time, when many ornate buildings were erected, including a turreted Rattenbury courthouse. There are 372 heritage buildings. Beached as a museum ship at Kaslo is the S.S. *Moyie*, the last of a fleet of stern-wheelers that once plied Kootenay Lake.

Right *Westbank, Okanagan Lake*; center *Prince George from Connaught Hill Park*; top *Prince Rupert*; facing page below and top right *Golden,* *Kicking Horse River*; facing page top left *Nelson on Kokanee Creek.*
Overleaf *An aerial view of the Canadian Rockies.*

GOLDEN
This was once the loading point for Upper Columbia sternwheelers. Completion of the C.P.R. in 1886 heralded the steamboat era when colourful little craft like the "Duchess" freighted to Columbia Lake and waypoints. Smelters built in 1904–05 were never blown in. Camps, steamers and smelters have gone, but Golden thrives because of its strategic location on the nation's major travel routes.
PROVINCE OF
BRITISH COLUMBIA
19   70

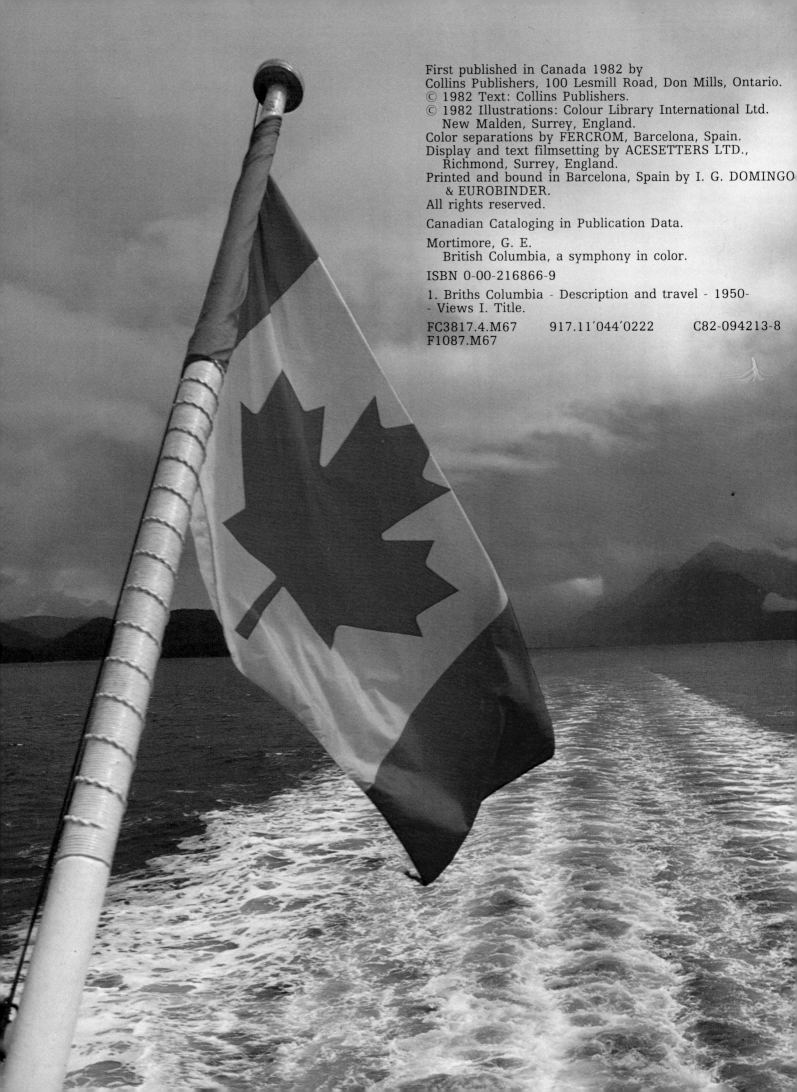

First published in Canada 1982 by
Collins Publishers, 100 Lesmill Road, Don Mills, Ontario.
© 1982 Text: Collins Publishers.
© 1982 Illustrations: Colour Library International Ltd.
 New Malden, Surrey, England.
Color separations by FERCROM, Barcelona, Spain.
Display and text filmsetting by ACESETTERS LTD.,
 Richmond, Surrey, England.
Printed and bound in Barcelona, Spain by I. G. DOMINGO
 & EUROBINDER.
Canadian Cataloging in Publication Data.

Mortimore, G. E.
 British Columbia, a symphony in color.
ISBN 0-00-216866-9

1. Briths Columbia - Description and travel - 1950-
- Views I. Title.

FC3817.4.M67   917.11′044′0222   C82-094213-8
F1087.M67